SERVING **OUR**
COUNTRY

U.S. ARMY

by Jill Sherman

AMICUS | AMICUS INK

Amicus High Interest is published by Amicus and Amicus Ink
P.O. Box 1329, Mankato, MN 56002
www.amicuspublishing.us

Library of Congress Cataloging-in-Publication Data
Names: Sherman, Jill, author.
Title: U.S. Army / by Jill Sherman.
Description: Mankato, Minnesota : Amicus, [2019] | Series: Serving our country | Includes index. | Audience: Grades K-3.
Identifiers: LCCN 2018002409 | ISBN 9781681515618 (library binding) | ISBN 9781681515991 (ebook) | ISBN 9781681523996 (pbk.)
Subjects: LCSH: United States. Army--Juvenile literature.
Classification: LCC UA25 .S543 2019 | DDC 355.00973--dc23
LC record available at https://lccn.loc.gov/2018002409

Photo Credits: iStock/zabelin cover; Shutterstock/Nikola m background pattern; iStock/DanielBendjy 2; Alamy/Oleg Zabielin 4; DVIDS/SSG Marcus Fichtl 7; DVIDS/HMC Josh Ives 8; DVIDS/Sgt. Stacy L. Pearsall 10–11; DVIDS/Sgt. Nathan Franco 12; DVIDS/U.S. Army photo by Sgt. Steven Galimore 15; Army Flickr/Staff Sgt Jason Epperson 16; DOD 18–19; Army Flickr/ Staff Sgt. Shawn Morris 21; Alamy/Militarist 22

Editor: Wendy Dieker
Designer: Aubrey Harper
Photo Researcher: Holly Young

Printed in China

HC 10 9 8 7 6 5 4 3 2 1
PB 10 9 8 7 6 5 4 3 2 1

TABLE OF CONTENTS

FIGHTING FORCES

War breaks out. The U.S. Army jumps into action. They are the soldiers that handle **land combat**. They fight at home and abroad. They defend our nation in times of need.

Force Fact
The Army was founded in 1775. It is older than the United States!

GEARED UP

On a mission, soldiers must blend in. Their clothing is **camouflaged**. The color and patterns match the landscape. They wear green in the jungle. They have tan for sandy areas.

Force Fact
Digital camouflage is a pattern of little squares. It can hide the soldiers really well.

COMBAT MISSIONS

Soldiers are ready to fight. They may need to destroy an enemy target. They might need to rescue a lost soldier. Army soldiers are ready for anything.

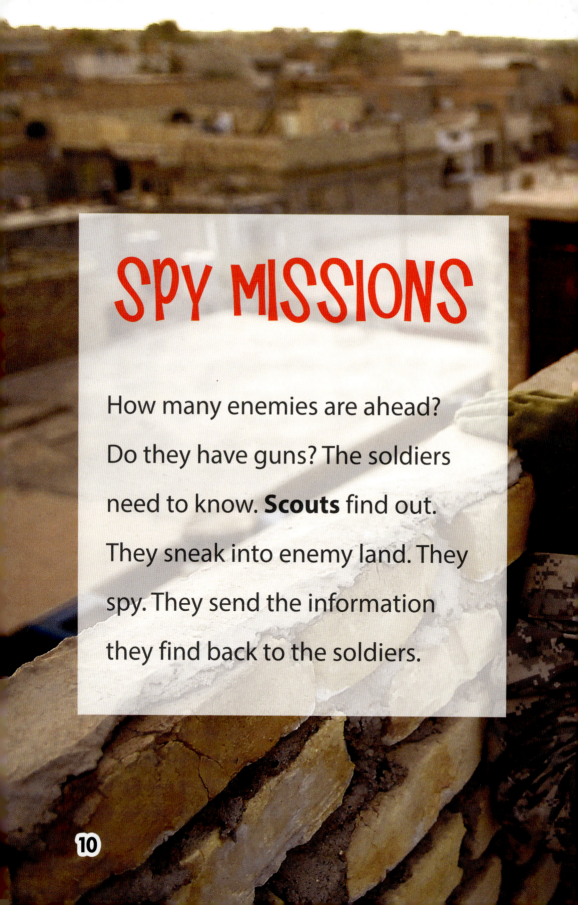

SPY MISSIONS

How many enemies are ahead? Do they have guns? The soldiers need to know. **Scouts** find out. They sneak into enemy land. They spy. They send the information they find back to the soldiers.

TANK POWER

Soldiers move into a dangerous area. They drive an Abrams tank. It has an armored **hull** to protect the soldiers inside. It has a big cannon. The tank packs a big punch.

Force Fact
The Abrams tank has a crew of four trained combat soldiers.

13

ROPE LANDING

Soldiers need to get to the battlefield fast. The Black Hawk helicopter takes them there. There is no room to land! That's ok. Soldiers **rappel** to the ground with ropes.

HELPING AROUND THE WORLD

The U.S. Army helps countries facing war. They help train local soldiers. They work to find **terrorists**. The Army helps rebuild towns and cities after war.

DISASTER RELIEF

The Army also helps after a disaster. A huge storm floods a city. The Army helps rescue stranded people. They build **dikes** to hold back water. The Army will help in an emergency.

ARMY STRONG

In times of war or peace, the U.S. Army serves America. They use weapons, tanks, and high-tech gear for their missions. Every day, the brave men and women of the U.S. Army keep us safe.

U.S. ARMY FAST FACTS

Founded: 1775

Members called: Soldiers

Main duty: Carry out combat missions from the ground

Members on active duty: 500,000

Motto: "This We'll Defend"

WORDS TO KNOW

camouflage Made of colors and patterns that work to hide the person or object.

dike A temporary or permanent wall built to hold back water during a flood.

hull The main body of a vehicle.

land combat Battles and fighting that take place on the ground, rather than at sea or in the air.

rappel To drop from a high place, such as an aircraft or rooftop, by rope.

scout A soldier trained to spy and gather information about a place before the rest of the soldiers arrive.

terrorists People who use violence and threats to frighten people into obeying.

LEARN MORE

Books

Boothroyd, Jennifer. *Inside the US Army*. Minneapolis: Lerner Books, 2017.

Grack, Rachel. *U.S. Special Forces*. Mankato, Minn.: Amicus, 2019.

Marx, Mandy. *Amazing US Army Facts*. Mankato, Minn.: Capstone Publishers, 2017.

Websites

Army Careers
www.goarmy.com

Official Home Page of the US Army
www.army.mil

INDEX

Every effort has been made to ensure that these websites are appropriate for children. However, because of the nature of the Internet, it is impossible to guarantee that these sites will remain active indefinitely or that their contents will not be altered.